A Familiar Stranger

May God richly
Bless you!
X
Sincerely,
Shirley Arline Fulford

A Familiar Stranger

Shirley Arlene Fulford

Ocean Isle Beach, North Carolina

Almar Books, Ocean Isle Beach, NC 28469 USA
www.almarbooks.com

First paperback edition, 2007

Printed in the United States

Library of Congress Control Number: 2007934897
ISBN-10: 0-9740983-6-1
ISBN-13: 978-0-9740983-6-4

Book and cover design: Sylvia Graham

Dedication

A true honest Christian can teach you much in silence, and a hypocrite can teach you nothing with a lot of fancy flowery words.

This book is dedicated first to my Lord and Savior and to His glorification, my beloved husband Robert, and all of my children and grandchildren.

It is my hope that my true life experiences will enable your faith to grow as mine has over the course of my lifetime. May you find, as I have, faith is the only real truth in life, and God is the root of all life.

Acknowledgements

Even way back then, I'd think broken things and broken hearted people were actually beautiful—a dog without a tail, a bird with a torn wing, handicapped people, disabled veterans, and even broken vases. To this day, I keep small broken pieces of jewelry, glass, earrings, beads, and display them on a glass shelf. When the lights or a candle shine on them, they look like radiant royalty. I always felt different from the rest of the world it seemed. I tried to look through rose colored glasses to find beauty somewhere.

I would like to thank Alice Tindall and Norma Chamberlin, and my early life role models for being great Sunday school teachers who imprinted their sincere, tremendous faith which still stands today in memory and song.

Many thanks to my sweet husband and children who offer constant support. They are and always will be my proudest, biggest fans.

A very special thanks to my closest and most wonderful friends, Betty, Sandra, (2) Peggys, Amelia, Nancy, Lucy, Billie-Anne, and Ruth. Your love and friendship has been a true encouragement.

Much appreciation to Jeff Brines who inspired me to write this book by saying it changed his life through changing his outlook. His confidence was a gift to me.

A special appreciation to Mark Smith who God sent to offer priceless help and advice.

Love and appreciation to Rhon and Alisa for the hours they put into this book.

May your goodness come back to you my dear family and friends.

A Familiar Stranger

There comes a time in everyone's life when they are faced with their own mortality. For me, it was after my "parents" deaths. My aunt and uncle had become my guardians, and grew to be my parents from God. Mother Walton had died of cancer and now it was my Father, Uncle Orville, of lung cancer.

I was on the long ride up from Coral Springs, Florida to my birthplace, New Jersey. Soon I would stand alone in Dutch Neck, New Jersey, where once life had been so full of energy and excitement. Now I would feel like I was home, but the whole world would be missing. The loneliness of that reality encompassed me, and melancholy with deep seated sadness set in. I pictured the church chimes playing favorite hymns, but the two most important people in my life would no longer be there to come home to. My mind drifted back to the past. What an interesting and amazing life it had been. I allowed past memory and reflection to comfort me in my sorrow by reliving it all.

My heart would always overflow at the very thought of New Jersey. Most of my earliest memories were of the beautiful seasons. The winters were truly like a living Christmas card, and Norman Rockwell himself could not have painted a more gorgeous landscape. Snow frosted the trees and there was the aroma of wood burning and crackling in the fireplaces. Spring brought lovely gardens alive with Lily of the Valleys, and flowers with beautiful fragrance. Because it was the Garden State, the land was rich for farming. Summer offered the Jersey shore with its wide, white, sandy beaches. The Atlantic Ocean was lined with bright beach toys, umbrellas, big shells, and rolling waves. Then I recall the gorgeous fall colors on the leaves of rich rust, green, gold, and burgundy hues. I proudly picked them up, shellacked them, then pasted each one in my scrapbook.

This is where my life and story began in a special place where God put me. Thank you, Father, I was blessed.

It was May 10, 1941, a Sunday morning. I was born to Mary Ella and Walter Paul Marriner. Shirley Arlene was my name. It was Mother's Day weekend, and I was mother's new appropriate gift. I was named after my mother's best friend who had been killed in a car accident a few weeks earlier. I have tried my best to honor my mother by often using both names, as she was apparently a very dear and special friend. I was proud to be her namesake.

My oldest brother Harry, sister Edee, middle brother Walter Paul II, and brother Marty were already born which made me the baby of the family. We ranged in age from newborn to ten. All except one would be total strangers for most of my life

When I was only two and a half years old, I lost most of my family. The five of us were scattered like little snowflakes in the wind. My mother died after she was stricken with a severe cold, bordering on pneumonia. The doctor gave her a shot of a new drug, and she developed a terrible reaction to it. She went into anaphylactic shock causing her throat to swell. Her breathing was labored as she told my brother, Walter Paul, she was going to the hospital and would not be coming back. She told him and my other brothers goodbye. She said I would go to stay with my aunt, her sister, until my father could find someone to care for us. My poor brothers saw their mother drive off, never to return. She was rushed to the hospital, but did not survive.

Soon my Aunt Edith and Uncle Orville would come for me. My brothers would see me waving and crying from my aunt's lap in an old Chevy, never to return either. Mother died in her early thirties. I have tried to imagine her courage and deep grief, gasping for air to speak through weakened breath to desperately place her children in a safe place. She did not know her baby would not be safe at all. She wanted the boys to stay with their Dad, and sister Edee was staying with my aunt already. I hurt now imagining her knowing she was dying, and wouldn't be here for her children.

Those were lean years. People were left devastated financially and emotionally from the Depression. Jobs were hard to find, and my father worked for the WPA Railroad which was set up by President Roosevelt. I wonder what he felt losing his wife, and his children being taken here and there.

Being too young to remember, I listened intently to what others told me about that day. I heard that my aunt told my Uncle Orville the day she got me that the three boys were saying, "take us we want to go too." It broke her heart she could only take Edee and me.

At age two and a half, I went to a precious community in Dutch Neck, New Jersey, so small they called it a village. It was a warm, close knit community with a loving environment. There were mostly elderly people who loved children, and most were farm people. The whole village centered around the old Presbyterian church. Soon, I would be labeled the new orphan in town. Many sweet, dear people seemed to adopt me into their hearts and lives. They showed so much love, I would feel happy there. This indicated God already had hold of my little hand by surrounding me with a lot of great Christian examples, and unforgettable Sunday school teachers. Between the ages of three and four, I was attending Sunday school, and spending time on the farm. Around four to five years of age, there would be trips to Asbury Park which were wonderful. It was an Atlantic Ocean front town with a long boardwalk. Point Pleasant was close by and sometimes we would go there on the boardwalk. It was a dream trip for a child. We would enjoy carousel rides, arcades, great smelling aromas of pizza, hot dogs and fries, and salt water taffy second to none!

My favorite treasure chest memory of those days was a little train in Point Pleasant. It ran from the boardwalk station all over the beach, way out near the sand dunes to the ocean on a little track. We would drive home through Freehold, NJ, and go to the Old Monmouth peanut brittle store.

We lived three doors down from the church, and my aunt would say it was the Lord calling Shirley to sermonette when the church bells called out. It would be true to say I was literally raised in that little country church. Strangely, at the age of four, I could hop up on the piano bench and play "Bye Bye Blackbird", my mother's favorite song, by ear. I was a little song bird and loved music as far back as I can picture. One thing I knew about my birth mother was that she played the organ and piano really well. She would keep me in her lap singing to me many days before her death I was told. When she was seventeen years old, she stood in church and accepted Jesus. I knew as a child she was in Heaven.

It was around this age, nearly five, that I would hear only pieces of my life, but could never gather enough information to make a complete picture. I would hear little hints about my family, but not enough to understand. I seemed to be a puzzle with many missing pieces. I would overhear comments such as my dad was an employee of WPA and a "disgrace," and why would he be proud of that? He was after all "lazy and useless." "He makes children then drops them off like stray cats for others to raise." My aunt said he was "immature and preferred to ice skate out on the lake" rather than be a parent. "It was a good thing Mary could cook" she said, because "he was a poor provider." A lot of feelings were derived from things I'd been told since I was too young to remember.

I was drawn like a magnet to the table to listen, but was immediately sent away. There was an unspoken rule to not ask questions about the father subject. I was truly and persistently in search of Shirley. I had no idea who I was or where I came from.

My mind would think, will my father grab me off the street and kidnap me? What lake were they talking about? Is it close by? What did my mother look like? Is my dad a bad person? Does he love me?

I never got the answers to my silent questions because it was an absolute closed subject. If I lit up with a curious question, that inquisitive candle would be very quickly blown out. What a mystery I was, who was I anyway? All I knew about me was

I loved animals, children and Jesus, and wanted nothing to hurt the above mentioned.

I would overhear how my mother loved seafood, and how she, Aunt Edith, and Aunt Helen were born in Belmar, New Jersey where they were raised on lobster and shrimp. They were close to the Atlantic Ocean. Oh how Mary loved oyster stew and those crackers from Trenton, especially made to compliment the soup. Then, I heard "Poor thing. I helped her get polio treatments. She was so beautiful, well brought up and sweet, she could have done better than that no good man. I tried to talk her out of marrying him, but she was stubborn and willfully would not listen. She married him against my advice anyway."

Whatever I did hear was generally positive towards my mom. Very early on, I became aware of the fact my father, Walter, was nearly hated and despised in that home. I was taught to be ashamed of him and my name, Marriner, the trash like name I carried. My aunt said it wasn't my fault I had bad blood. My little mind raced to fifth gear. Was I sick? Did I have a disease? Would I die? Was I going to a doctor? Whatever I was, I must not be anything to be proud of.

My aunt was not able to have children and she just adored me. I know she wanted the very best for me. She loved her sister, my mother, with all of her heart. She had a lot of responsibility as a child. My grandmother Gravatt was mentally ill. My Aunt Helen had a brain tumor, and my mom was frail from polio. My grandfather, her dad, worked hard as a farmer; therefore, all of the household duties fell on my poor Aunt Edith. She had to take care of everyone and everything. She would clean, cook, and be care taker for her mother and sisters. She could not attend school regularly. She would have to bring school work home in order to take care of her family. She was exceptionally bright. At seventeen years old she went to Trenton State Teachers and Business School, graduated and obtained a good position in a bank. She stayed there until her retirement.

Aunt Edith had a very big, wonderful, loving heart. She was a very good lady, and an extremely caring and astute business woman. To be in her presence was a joy and pleasure because of her ready smile. She was deeply generous. Her brown eyes were warm and kind. She always gave a big beautiful smile. If I inherited anything from her, it was her funny bone gene and roaring sense of humor. Many laugh lines crossed my face with Aunt Edith. No matter what my circumstances, she would bring a big smile. I loved her dearly.

Uncle Orville had a complex personality. He was a good man and a very hard worker. He was kind, yet grumpy and grouchy. He was strict yet decent. Uncle Orville was a serious man and had limited patience with children. He had a gruff voice and a critical tongue. He was smart and had an attic full of National Geographic magazines. He educated himself about what was going on in the world. He listened to Walter Winchell and Gabriel Heater on the radio daily. I credit him for my early interest in reading, and he certainly taught the importance of an education. When he was home, he would be reading, listening to the radio or on the ham operator radio contacting people.

It wasn't that he did not love. He did, but he was very reserved to the point where you couldn't easily feel his love. He didn't express it well. I was scared to death I would make him angry. I remember trying so hard to win Uncle Orville's heart so I would be loved and accepted there. It seemed he was not overly thrilled to suddenly become a substitute parent in his middle age. He, after all, had not been a natural parent and was a true workaholic. God knows he tried. If I fell, he put salve on my scraped knees, and tightened up my little roller skates. He would run beside me as I learned to ride my bike.

His occupation was in plumbing and heating which he learned as a young boy. He worked hard to feed and clothe me. Both he and Aunt Edith were generous. They were the only parents I had. I thought before God, anything I felt they were wrong about was tempered with deep love for both of them.

In Florida driving on Interstate 95, I felt his death with such agonizing grief. I realized how much he meant to me.

I never wanted for the material things of life in my childhood. I shuffled through pictures where I was always dressed up like a doll. I wore lace, velvets, angora, and little ribbons that matched every outfit. My greatest need was on the inside, an emotional need to fit in and feel secure. I always felt on the outside like the lost child. I tried hard to be obedient and tried hard to please.

I would at times be alone but felt completely safe in my caring community. I would skate, dance, twirl, and run around the yard with pretty colored streamers held to a piece of cardboard with rubber bands holding it all together. At home I'd sing, tap and scarf dance. I loved to play hopscotch and jump rope.

I was five years old and all excited about going to school. Most of the people in town were elderly, and I had only one playmate. I remember thinking I would have lots of new friends to meet.

My sister Edee and I were nine years apart. She had lots of friends. There was such an age span, we did not share a lot of things until we got older. She was a wonderful sister, always so good and sweet to me. She was very protective, always loyal and there for me. I know when we lost our parents it was a deep grieving loss for her too.

On some days, my newly adopted Grammie and Auntie Vi (Uncle Orville's mother and sister) would take care of me. Aunt Edith would pay them to baby-sit, and apparently from the early years, I was there through the week while my aunt and uncle worked. I bonded to Grammie and Auntie Vi easily. I simply worshiped those two women. They took care of me through chicken pox, measles and mumps. They were deeply loving and kind. I felt very special to them.

Grammie lived on an old farm, and the cooking and the love made it a haven for me. I loved the rain, feather beds, tin roof, and lots of homemade jams and jellies on the shelves. I had my own little room. Pop Pop (Uncle Orville's father) was my hero. He was warm, funny and loving. I was a little sun beam in his eyes. He built me a swing. I loved swinging high out on the old oak tree. I had a tea set and a very antagonistic crow which would swoop down, grab my little china cup and sit up on the telephone wires seemingly enjoying my tears of frustration. It taunted me with a wicked eye. Pop Pop would rescue me by scaring the crow away. He would retrieve my tea cup that the crow dropped while flying away.

Auntie Vi went to school with my mother, Mary. They were best friends. She never married or had a child, but she was the most nurturing woman I had ever met. She lives vividly in my heart. She was gentle, sweet and an angel, and I was her princess.

Back then life was more comfortable and trusting. Doors were left open and not locked. Everyone knew each other. No one thought about security measures, because not a soul thought they had to. This is what I fell victim to. I simply had a child's wide-eyed trust, and believed in the goodness of everyone in my community. I felt perfectly safe. Neighbors were practically family back then. I would call them aunt and uncle as a term of respect and endearment.

September would soon be here when I would enter kindergarten. I was approaching five and a half years old. I was by myself at home. My sister was fourteen years old and out with friends. I wanted to go outside and play.

Before my aunt went to work, she would tell me, "Shirley, if you need anything, run to the neighbors." It seemed I had many people looking out for me because everyone knew me. I would be roller skating on the sidewalk up at the church or on my bike ringing the bell all over town. I was always in clear view.

On this particular day, I slammed the screen door. The big hook popped up over the circle hook and fastened to lock me out. It was an unusually hot and humid day. Soon I needed water and to use the bathroom. I hurried back to my door and discovered I was locked out.

I ran to the house next door, to my aunt and uncle's good friends. If memory serves me right, the neighbor's wife was bedridden upstairs and ill.

A s soon as I entered the house, he grabbed me. He slammed me hard up against the wall. I suffered a huge bump on the back of my head. It was bleeding. He pinned me there and heavily molested me for a long time. He was breathing heavily and smelled of liquor or beer. To this day I can not stand the smell of alcohol. I was so scared and frightened, I wet my panties. It was humiliating. He sensed and could see the fear very strongly. He told me if I ever told this to my aunt and uncle, I would be sent to a state home for children where I would be starved, beaten and frozen to death. At the age of only five, I remember he said, "They don't want you here. You are not even adopted." I did not know what adopted meant, but I did understand the part about not being wanted. I was told we had a secret and I better keep it that way or I would go to the unwanted children's home. I believed him.

My head bled a little, and I lied saying I fell on the concrete going down a hill and hit the back of my head while roller skating. But, I had to be brave. He certainly knew the right words to put total fear in my heart, because I would never tell. I recall feeling unable to breath during the abuse.

At times on the trip back from Florida, I was jolted with memories. It was like it happened yesterday, reliving the sense of weakness, helplessness, shame and thoughts about how terribly scared I was of him. I'd was back in my childhood in my mind, even though we were on Florida highways.

With my uncle's personality and my being so intimidated by him, I have always felt he never would have believed me anyway. That one day in my life violated me so deeply that it would haunt me for the rest of it. It killed my innocence and self-esteem. I had no one to tell or protect me. The weight of carrying shame on my small shoulders all the days of my childhood and into my adult life was overwhelming. My gruff uncle's best friend was this perverted man. They had no idea.

He would stalk me at night. My sister and I shared a room. I could see him at night, undressed with the light of his cigarette exposing his bareness, looking over trying to get a peep of me or my young teen sister. His bedroom was directly across from ours up on the second floor. He was like a lion waiting to trap his prey. I made everything dark and ran in and pulled the curtains as tight as I could. A sick feeling of guilt like I might get sick to my stomach was my usual night time routine. I would tell my aunt I felt sick with a tummy ache and often I would sleep downstairs. My sweet sister would try to take care of me and compensate for the loss of my mother, but I still wished I had my mother to protect me from this man.

Thank God I had the church three doors down. I loved to sit in children's church and hear Reverend Ben Singer tell how much Jesus loved little children. My aunt was strong on my attendance. It was around this time I started calling her Mother. She seemed to embrace the title comfortably.

On Mother's Day as soon as I walked into the church foyer, I would be handed a flower that represented the dead mother, and that would really hurt. Everyone seemed to have the living carnation if they were young. But, one wonderful thing my aunt did, for which I am extremely grateful, she took me on many Mother's Day Sunday's with a little basket of pretty flowers or a plant to place by the stone of my mother's grave. Then she would say, "Shirley, I don't want you to ever forget the lady who gave you your life." That showed me her heart clearly. She didn't try to replace or upstage my mother in my heart. I would place my little flowers and try so very hard, over and over, to visualize what she looked like under the ground.

I was told my mother was very pretty in her purple dress that was given to her in death by my aunt Edith. She said it was a beautiful purple dress with delicate lace. On that day, I adopted purple as my favorite color. Not having seen a picture of my mom, I just couldn't see a face. She was a person I didn't know even though she carried me nine months and gave birth. I saw my aunt's attention to her grave and I knew she was loved greatly.

Because I was hurting from my neighbors attack, I would avoid going anywhere near there. I became very close to Jesus and I attended church through the week including Wednesday prayer. I went to Sunday school and worship service all through my childhood. I am sure church was the thing that saved my sanity. This is how my faith grew. The church influence was my lighthouse of hope. Jesus was my friend. He died for me. I was an unusually spiritual child. My child-like faith came from seeing and hearing. In my lowliness, I would look up to the Lord through rainbows and clouds, and learn from wonderful models who were true and gracious God fearing people. People such as my two aunts, grandmother, and Sunday school teachers were perfect role models. I painted pictures of the Lord in His purple robe. I loved to sing little Christian songs. I had certificates for perfect attendance between the ages of three to five. My light faith became very strong. My little light grew to a big one.

Uncle Orville was a fireman. Within a day, firemen would be his pallbearers and a fire truck part of his funeral. He was a proud American. As a child, I would stand watching the Veterans and people holding flags in parades. Uncle Orville stood for country, God, and community. He loved those small town parades.

Poor mother was not a domestic goddess at all. I was raised on church banquets. Pancakes, Italian sausage, and fish chowder were all I remember her cooking. We took lots of trips to the diner for supper. Her love and passion was for banking, not cooking. Fortunately, and to my delight, she loved sweets. Our house was always stocked with bake sale goodies and the candy dish was always full. What I loved about the farm were those terrific meals from the old coal stove, shelves full of jam preserves, Thanksgiving dinners made from scratch, and desserts that would be beyond delicious. Grammie always made the best gingerbread men. She was a great cook.

My greatest happiness would be when I could escape the child molester and be with Auntie Vi and Grammie on the farm. Pop Pop was the only man

I trusted. I had just kissed him goodnight. He had a massive stroke and died on the eve of his fiftieth wedding anniversary. I was completely devastated. I just cried and cried missing him. Grammie, in her deepest sorrow, sat near me and made clothespin dolls to help ease the pain. She was tuned into my needs. I would have stayed there forever, but on the weekends I had to go home.

I would look normal, but was being destroyed on the inside. Mother and Father would play cards on Saturday evenings with him, the abuser. They would alternate homes, and sometimes I would have to go next door to his house and face my molester. When we were at his house, he made snacks. My aunt would tell me to go into the kitchen and help bring things back to drink and snack on. He would always use the opportunity to grab me in private places or expose himself. You could hear the others talking in the other room. He knew we were alone. He'd ask in a whisper to touch quickly, and then he'd go back in laughing and playing the perfect host.

I would feel deeply depressed, scared, nervous, and upset. He would be so bold as to pull me up on his lap, and put rings on my fingers from a White Owl cigar box. My aunt and uncle would just marvel over his kindness towards me. I would go home in shame, and then attend children's church the next morning. This would be repeated over and over.

Finally, I was ready for kindergarten. I was all dressed up in a red plaid dress, red ribbons in my pig tails, red leather shoes, and a cute little lunch box of red plaid to match. I remember being proud of my new red shoes. I looked like a typical child but entered kindergarten with a wisdom and knowledge far beyond my years to which the adults in my world were oblivious. I was so messed up by my experiences that I could barely even function at school.

My aunt and uncle cared about my education. They would be upset that I was not applying myself. It wasn't a lack of application. I was day dreaming most days and could not concentrate or focus. Was it my fault? Did I make him do that to me? I felt worthless with self loathing. I felt alone and abandoned by my father. I remember having a hard time connecting to God because of my own father. Did my father, Walt, hate me? Why didn't he write, call or come to see me?

School was hard because it required a lot of concentration and I was a dreamer. I didn't even know I was smart until I went to college years later and got straight A's. My intelligence came more from reading, painting, art and crafts, and creative things. I always loved beautiful dolls. I would struggle with math, but I could make attractive bouquets from leaves, honeysuckle and baby roses. I could design crafts, and make nice Christmas candies. I'd take white birch, make a log, and put candles in two holes, then place holly, gold painted pine cones, and pine needles to level the bottom. It was placed up on our fireplace. Uncle Orville would always help me out in the garage with all my creations. I could sing and dance well but couldn't concentrate in school. I did love Jesus, animals and children. Once I was chosen to play Mary, the mother of Jesus, in a candlelight service. I had long dark hair and in my mind I was Mary that night. It was an unforgettable memory. At the time it gave me so much needed self esteem. I sang all over in weddings, funerals, and parties.

I was really God fearing and would worry about God being upset with me for my lying about the well kept secret. I was taught to be honest, have integrity and never ever lie. Mother was death on lying.

I was seven or eight years old now and loved the winters. I was very much a fashion girl and would carry my white figure skates to the nearest lake wearing a turtle neck sweater, white knee high poinsettia socks with holly trim, a little skirt, scarf, and hat set and off I'd fly. I'd feel exhilarated by the sound of my blades cutting over the ice while making a path of my own. I would pretend I was the star of the Ice Capades in New York. I would spin, jump and glide and use fantasy as a crutch, because real life wasn't that glamorous. I was a good skater and well practiced. My mind could make things beautiful even if my circumstances couldn't. I could do tricks on roller and ice skates like you wouldn't believe. I'd make snow angels, and forts and write my name thousands of times in the snow with big icicle.

I'd ride as far as I could on my bike because then I wouldn't be home next door to the one I was most afraid of in life. I was scared to death of him my entire childhood, and he couldn't escape my mind because he was always so close. I was petrified they would somehow find out. My aunt was sharp and practically nothing got past her. Sometimes I could smile and cover my true emotions, but other times I thought I would burst with sadness and fear. It was hard to fake but I had to and I did. I had a lot of happy days, too, laughing and playing with my friends.

My life was balanced but the questions seemed unstoppable back then. Where were my brothers? Did my brothers miss me? Why didn't my grandparents call or write? Had they all forgotten me? I had a lot of time to think during all those quiet snow days.

I was still as confused as ever. Mother's preaching "hate your father", and Reverend Ben Singer preaching "honor your father and mother." Reverend Ben Singer spoke all about love and forgiveness. Did that mean I had to forgive the man next door, God?

I would sit on the porch and ask God to introduce me to my mother when I die someday. As an adult I still ask that prayer.

The questions continued. What could Dad have done that was so terrible Mother hated him? One day my brother, Walter Paul, came to see me. It was brief, and I was in awe but we never mentioned it again. It was a Saturday morning. Mother was cordial and happy to see him, but Father was reserved. Once my brother Harry had hitch hiked all the way to come see me. Father said, "Go back where you came from. You are not welcome here." Were they afraid of losing me? I don't know.

I was around ten or eleven years old. My father could be so rude, but about the time I wondered if he cared about me at all, he would do something incredibly sweet and memorable—like the time on my tenth birthday. I woke up still sleepy and heard Father calling me. I went out on the back porch and there he was ringing the bell on my newly painted blue stinger bike. It had a new white basket on it and I could not mistake the love in his heart and eyes when he gave that bike of my sister's to me. He put on new tires and had flowers in my basket. God showed me at different times that I really was loved by him a lot. Heaven knows he truly became my father. Tears well in my eyes at the memory of that day. He was and always will be my father, the one the Lord gave to me.

I guess my sense of humor was a survival gift from above. I had a flash of my aunt who would make funny faces at me through the window. She'd be washing and could be so child like, silly, and goofy. Around twelve or thirteen years old, I had a sweet memory that was so precious—snow flurries, icy sidewalks, frosted windows, Christmas trees, wreathes at each home, and chimes playing at church, Mother and I walking arm in arm up to the Sunday school building. We had on boots, slipping and sliding, and holding each other up. We were wrapped up in fur hats and gloves. We were elated to be together. Mother was the biggest kid in town at Christmas. I truly believe she relived her empty childhood vicariously through me and my sister, Edee. Maybe that's why she kept me? She needed me? She couldn't have children. Did she need our love? She always said we brought them joy.

Grammie was a blessing, too. I wouldn't have made it without her old time remedies. Once I fell on a barbed wire, and tore open my leg. She picked me up and dressed that leg like a skilled surgeon. She just sprang into action if I got hurt. She'd help eliminate boils, treat insect bites, and rid me of colds. She used mustard plaster, and cherry salve on skinned knees like Father did, and she gave one tablespoon of Vicks to swallow for the flu. Canker sores were gone with something I called, "Purple Torture." It most certainly worked. Grammie lived to be one hundred years old, never having a tetanus shot or penicillin. She was amazing. While sewing, she didn't even need glasses.

As our car headed towards the Virginia border, I looked in the mirror. My sense of humor couldn't rise above my heartbreak over Father's death. I was no stranger to sorrow. I know tons of tears had crossed my face, the throbbing, sobbing kind that empty you dry and leave you with dry sockets and a headache. I could generally give a big smile away, covering up all the pain with a great acting performance. Of course I always had a lot of laugh lines on my face as well. Seeing my reflection, I ran my finger to my eye from my temple trying to wipe the pain away. Today, no smiles could break through the unbearable loss I was feeling. Today, my face of thirty-eight years had only dark circles and a pale look. It seemed I felt love and pain magnified. Did everybody hurt this bad?

Both Father and Mother Walton taught me about having a responsibility to give back. We were to help others and serve. Yes, they were both good souls and good people. I was raised with a lot of pride in flags, and God Bless America patriotic times. The training I received helped me to do something good with my life. I had a strict upbringing, and I did love Jesus. I felt that responsibility. Christianity didn't mean vanity. I was adamant about not wanting to ever be self righteous. I had a ministry spirit and felt the responsibility of it. My parents words echoed back to help the poor.

I looked out the window and saw the "Welcome to Delaware" sign. Soon, possibly tomorrow, I would be standing in New Jersey in the driveway of the cute little bungalow I was raised in. Father and Uncle Jay, his brother, built it. It was a doll house, cozy, and very charming like an English cottage with maple furniture.

I thought back to the day I was about thirteen years old, and was looking for crayons or markers in the drawer. I saw an envelope with my name on it. It was my birth certificate. It was strange studying my birth certificate my parents had signed and realizing that they were complete strangers to me.

Between the ages of fourteen and sixteen, youth fellowship was my social life. I was old enough to start high school. I was a really popular girl now and had lots of friends. I loved to dance and went to proms a lot, but when it came down to excelling, that old ghost would haunt me. I had so much fear of failure.

I attended Princeton High School and it was a great school. It was the third in the nation in those days. My humor would be my defense mechanism to cope at the time. I had put most of my energy into being popular, as that was my greatest need to fit in and to belong. I was sociable, lovable, and fun.

In my year book it read, "Always laughing, antici-pates weekends gleefully." By then I had learned as a latch key kid how to lock myself in. I was a fierce protector of myself. I'd had years to get skilled at covering up and stuffing down past secrets. I was good at the cover up, but bad about healing my inside emotions. On the outside you couldn't see the pain. I was kind of a social recluse and only trusted me. Throughout those years, there was a voice inside telling me no matter what, I could run into Jesus' open arms and find comfort there. I had many lessons to learn and learning from the hard roads seemed to be my destiny. I learned from my childhood a great truth. A true, honest Christian can teach you much in silence and a hypocrite can teach you nothing with lots of fancy, flowery words. Those great examples gave me strength

Poor Father quickly took second place when I turned sweet sixteen in 1955, and in the library found my first love, Bobby. For me, it was a heart-throb issue, and was the same for him. I wore his ring, and was obsessed twenty-four hours a day. Father would tease, "Bobby today and Billy next month." I was in love, crazy in love. Eventually, the physical would be pursued. I held off until almost eighteen years old, and was scared to death I'd lose him. All the willing girls wanted him. After all, he was the cutest boy in high school.

Unfortunately, his first love was his sports car. I was so fragile in the love department that I wanted a firm commitment of marriage after graduation. He talked about an engagement ring. When payday came around, he never had money for the ring, but always had enough to fix up my rival, the old car. I got jealous, and just as impulsive as I could be, broke up with him.

I rebounded to an old high school friend. I was so needy to be someone's everything. He was a handsome, sophisticated, intelligent man full of charm and charisma. His father was a police sergeant on the Princeton force. His family had an established floral shop in the town of Princeton where he was born. My parents had an anniversary, and he came out to Dutch Neck to deliver the flowers I had ordered. He had traveled to Europe and was very classy. He would take me to a French restaurant and order Vichyssoise. I'd have to ask him what it meant. I wasn't from a world of social life and experience. He and I had gone to Princeton High School, and we were casual friends

He took me out twice, and then on our third evening out, he brought gardenias and beautiful silver earrings. We went to meet his grandparents in Point Pleasant, New Jersey. As we were coming toward Princeton Junction, he pulled over into a parking lot which happened to be a bar and grill.

I got a little panicked because I was terrified of drinking. Suddenly, under the lamplight he pulled out a diamond engagement ring, and I screamed, "Yes, I'll marry you!" I accepted a marriage proposal three days after our first date.

He fell truly and deeply in love, and I'm sure I actually was the only woman he did ever love. During this time, I was in nursing school at Lambert House in Princeton Hospital. He wanted me to quit school and said I could go back later. I was always subservient and obedient as I was really intimidated by men. In my immaturity, I made sure our engagement announcement was on the first page of the social section of the paper. I had hoped my true love would see it, feel bad, and regret not getting the ring for me. This was a classic example of hurting myself the most, him, my high school boyfriend, and our parents by not letting God guide me to what I still believed was the right path for a happy future.

The look on Mother and Father's face was one of sheer horror when I came home with the ring on my finger, waking them up saying, "I'm engaged." I was totally thrilled. Catching the sparkle on my ring from Mother's lamp on her nightstand was thrilling. Father had a coughing fit, and I don't think it was from cigarettes. For some reason, they let me be an independent thinker and didn't force their opinions on me, but their faces said it all.

We were married in beautiful Trinity Episcopal Church in Princeton. When my father walked me down the isle, he looked as if he was attending a wake along with my mother. They acted detached and non-supportive. My husband's family had to get my dress, shoes, and flowers. Mother Walton did take me to buy a new coat so I'd be warm. We got married in January. It was very cold. Obviously, they felt it was a big mistake and it should have been Bobby. They both liked and approved of him.

My sister attended our wedding but Mother and Father were so puritanical and strict, and they didn't speak to her because she had gotten a divorce. She was hurt and sad because no one spoke to her. I felt like taffy pulled between the three of them. I didn't want to be disloyal to anyone, and I loved all three.

I would notice that my new husband would have a drink when we were out for dinner, but I thought this meant he was polished and suave, and drank in social situations. I was not wise in this area. I had no idea he had a very serious drinking problem. When he drank, his personality would change. Sober he was a gentleman with a sweet and loving demeanor. After three drinks, he became a completely different personality. There was way too much stress, noise, and chaos. Even though he'd be a great husband in other areas, such as bringing home flowers, beautiful clothing, and charms for a bracelet, the drinking would ruin what we might have built on. I was tired of being ignored every night. I needed more love than most, and wasn't getting the attention I craved since he'd be up all night drunk. It made me nervous and frightened, and I could not stand being around someone so out of control.

Most nights would be spent pulling out cigarette burnings on the sofa and mattress from the holes burned in the sheets. I became afraid of him. The slightest issue could set him off, and at times I'd have to run to my sister. I respected the man, my husband, but I hated the drinking. I didn't want any man throwing verbal abuse at me ever again.

Through all of this, there was my Heavenly Father who sent into my life what would be the best and most beautiful gifts. My daughter, Tara Lynne, came first in 1962. I was in intensive care after her birth as I had developed toxemia, pre-eclampsia, and my kidneys shut down. My blood pressure soared. We were not supposed to make it by medical standards, but God brought us through.

My son Rhon was born in 1964, and six years later my youngest daughter, Darise Alene. Because of them I have known the love of God as my Father, and the joy and fulfillment of being someone's mother. My angels, all three! They are my deepest pride and happiness. What a warm feeling to know they all do love the Lord.

From Father and Mother's teaching and my New Jersey years, I taught them to be giving, understanding, and to give back to God. I wanted them to grow up knowing even through loss and pain, life was still very wonderful and beautiful. If I could have taken a forever pill, I would have taken two, because I did love life madly, intensely, and passionately—with a purple passion!

My children's dad, when not drinking, was thoughtful and good to me. He bought special charms for my bracelet, fifteen in all for anniversaries and Christmas, and one for each child on the eve of their birth. It was so sad, because he was an extraordinary person. Alcohol destroyed him. I wasn't stable enough to help and actually enabled him by covering up a lot. I thought love could heal anything. I probably grew to love him. I was sad because I wanted to save him, but you can't save a person from himself.

All through my twenties I'd be questioning who I was, and where was my family? I still could not make peace with it. I was still a mystery in a dark closet. I knew I was a mother now, but who was my children's mother, really? What was the ancestry and background of my family members? Were there serious medical problems?

Now, I was on my way to New Jersey to my father's service. I knew I could never hurt them by trying to find my immediate family while they lived. It would feel like I wasn't honoring them. If my tears had any power, I'd will them back to life. They were deeply important to me.

Our first born, Tara, got very sick from allergies, double pneumonia, and upper respiratory infections. We moved from New Jersey to Ft. Lauderdale, Florida where she would be in a better climate. When we left New Jersey, Mother was in agony from the excruciating pain of cancer. It seemed like Florida was so far away.

I had such a driven need to be loved, and often when the dear Lord had a hold of me, I would let go and enter into the world seeking this love. I did not, with willful intent, be rebellious or disobedient. I was just driven to find this attention, as if I'd been starved for it all my life. My mind and heart could not stand the thought of my poor mother lying in a New Jersey hospital bed dying slowly each day. I felt devastated. I was terribly lonely. I missed my parents. Instead of looking upward, my eyes were on me and my miserable circumstances. It overwhelmed me.

So, skipping right into the wrong path again, and being easily led by Satan because he knew how to use my insecurities to bait me, he placed a man in my life. At this vulnerable time, this man promised me the sun, moon and stars, listened to my story of the past, and totally convinced me he would carry my life and that of my children to new heights. It all looked good when I was depressed and starving for support and someone held a banquet within my reach. Hungry for love, I was longing to find a good man. I jumped right into an affair, fully persuaded I would finally be treated like a queen.

In an unplanned, careless moment I got pregnant. You have never seen a queen lose her throne so quickly! I was offered enough money for an abortion while he slipped right out of my life, hiding behind his family, leaving me to face my insanely jealous and angry husband alone. I had to look at my three sweet children, and if you could die from shame and fear, I would have. The pain was so great. I suddenly felt beneath my husband's feet, and he definitely made me feel that way. I had run to the man in the affair. He saw my needy heart and used me. I was to blame, too. Where was my spirit? Where were my morals?

With all I had endured, I had never suffered so much grief as when I decided to end my pregnancy. I had an abortion. I felt truly forced to do it, but I did have a choice. I always felt powerless around men. I let them pressure me to make that choice. I gave them all my power and strength. I put a man before God, and I knew better. I was a puppet, and a man could pull my strings.

We were now in Delaware, approaching the Delaware Memorial Bridge, and I was reliving the abortion experience. Oh, I want to tell other women and young ladies: Do not choose abortion. You will suffer the rest of your life with sadness in your soul. Every Mother's Day, I ache and hate myself.

I ended up in a dirty, dumpy clinic in the Bronx, New York. It was horrible. It had dirty sinks full of blood, and thrown down gloves. We were all lined up like cattle in our so-called hospital gowns, given a shot in our hip, and then as we'd weaken, we'd be put in a room where the procedure took place. I was shaking and scared.

I didn't know that my baby had a heartbeat, brain cells, and a form. Your baby is broken in pieces and violently sucked out. "Oh God," I thought. "I don't belong here." There was a little thirteen year old aborting at five months, and she was hysterical. My heart reached out to help her through this horrible experience. "Oh my God, what have I done?" I thought. I had to fly over my dying mother in New Jersey to go to Kennedy Airport and get a taxi the Bronx. It was so humiliating.

I thought in the car on the way to Mother's funeral someday I must write a book. If it stopped one woman from aborting, my life would be an example by learning from my mistakes. The experience would be worth something.

When I flew back to Florida, my husband strongly resented me and felt betrayed. I had hurt him badly. I filed for divorce and won custody of my children. He must have loved me once, because he fought the divorce and begged me not to leave. I knew he would hold this over my head and torture me about it from that point on. I felt so bad about myself, and I did not feel good enough for him at that time. I wanted his respect for having three of his children, but he was unable to give it after this betrayal. He was very bitter. This was my bottom in life. No one could go lower. Even though I would plunge to the lowest depth, I never wanted out of life. Not ever. God had not given life for me to end it. He gives and He takes. I belonged to Him, not me. Life is still beautiful, no matter what. It's a precious gift. A lot of pain we cause ourselves because we give Satan control.

I was deep in suffering over my abortion, and would see my baby being killed by me over and over in my dreams. Later in life, I held a teddy bear, rocked and held the paws around my neck, rubbed its back, and dedicated my baby to Jesus. I lit a candle and had a memorial service. My husband couldn't forgive it. Thank God Jesus could and He did. I know He did. Maybe someday I could finally forgive myself, and one day I'll hold my baby in Heaven.

My ex-husband moved back up to New Jersey where he would be attending Uncle Orville's funeral the next day. He placed three yellow roses, my father's favorite, at the graveside to represent our children. The good Lord knows he was a sweetheart, and very sensitive when sober. He honestly was so lovable and likeable. No one could help but care about him. Did I still have feelings? I'm not sure if I loved him more than I even knew. Every time the song, "The Way We Were" would play, I would think of him. Was I ever sure about love? Did I even know what love truly was? I definitely had low self esteem issues throughout life. I really did not know the depth of my feelings. I guess I did miss his romantic ways. There were always flowers, candles and dancing. This was probably what attracted me in the first place. I was with him for fourteen years of my life.

Well, here we are turning off Exit 8 from the New Jersey Turnpike. This exit takes you to Hightstown, and then a little drive to Dutch Neck, my sweet village and home. As I had predicted, I felt so lost at home without them.

I paid my respect to my father, grieved with my sister, and took the long trip back to Florida. No clouds lifted. I was feeling very down. I was crying and depressed for months and so lonely for them. I couldn't cover up the deep pain. The thought kept haunting me. Was Father saved? Did he know Jesus in his heart? I remember seeing him go to church only twice - once at my sister's wedding, and the other time at my wedding. Maybe he went for a couple Easter Sundays of my childhood.

When we got back to Florida after the funeral, my children and I moved on to a life of our own. It was not a good one. We struggled with extreme poverty and I sold nearly everything including furniture, wedding rings, and china in order to live. I had to do something at home to support us. I started taking care of other people's children, church people, lawyers, doctors, and neighbors. I would clean houses on the weekends. In God's forgiveness, He returned my child to me by sending other children I could love and teach about Jesus. I lost my baby, but He had mine in Heaven, and gave me His on earth to nurture, love, and enjoy while caring for them. I cared for many children - babies, after school children, and special needs kids. I am a strong child advocate. I have stood outside of a car where kids were left unattended and alone to protect a stranger's children. The elderly are like children. They need hugs, shoes laces tied, and prayer. They are really little ones too. I have cared for many elderly people. I was raised with them and they are special to me.

We had to go through many frustrations and disappointments because there was never ever enough money. I would cry when I could not afford an Easter basket for my youngest child. Christmas was hard. We had been thrown out by our landlord because I was one month behind in the rent. He kept what little we had, and changed the locks. We lost the barest necessities we had. My kids were broken hearted. They lost their favorite toys and treasures. I had the precious charm bracelet on my arm, the one thing I adored. I loved the bracelet so much, but sometimes I had to sell a charm for food or Christmas gifts. The fifteen charms were worth little to someone else, but millions to me. One charm was a little house with two hearts on the sofa, one an oyster shell with a pearl, and one a Christmas tree of jewels. It was truly lovely.

I explained to the children that it was no sin to be poor. I worried about my children and the bills. With all of our problems, I was still a good person and didn't do anything indecent, drink, or pop pills. I tried to be strong. One thing I did make sure of was that my children knew Jesus. I took them to church and Sunday school. At points of desperation and right on time, God sent Christians from church to provide Christmas trees, turkeys, a house full of gifts, cookies, and goodies for us.

What completely shocks me is that my children tell me that being poor made them stronger. It was actually a blessing because they did not have anything handed to them, and what they acquired on their own they truly appreciated. I would tell others, just hold on, look up and pick up. You'll be so surprised. God will bless you in the hard times. Trust and wait. I had to sell diamonds to help us through, but I learned that we didn't need expensive things. I keep my treasures in my mind and heart where no one can steal them or where I would have to lose them

Soon the four of us settled in an apartment with basically nothing. By now I was tired and holding it together by just a thread. I felt worn out and weak at times. For a few days I was down with the flu and could not go to the doctor. I heard the door bell ring and there stood my neighbor with a pot of chicken and rice and a card. His children and mine had played together after school, and my children must have mentioned I was sick. I certainly was surprised and asked him to come in for a cup of coffee. When we talked, he told me of the difficulty he was having raising three sons by himself, and how he was divorcing. He had to work and had no one to care for his children. I recall feeling so sorry for the burden he seemed to be carrying.

The neighbor pursued me with a lot of care and kindness. Before long we started to plan our future together. We had plans to leave Florida and go to North Carolina which was his home state. He said he knew he could find work there.

One day his wife came to Florida and discovered I was in his life. Apparently, she had no idea they were not happily married and planned to be with her family. He had sent her a letter saying, "Don't return, it's over." She was in complete shock.

We packed up all eight of us and moved to Raeford, North Carolina. We got married and at times we were a big happy family. The kids seemed to get along great and we had fun. Later, I hurt for the boys' mom because she was truly a wonderful person. The Lord made us close friends even though we had been involved in really sensitive circumstances. Sometimes we would have the boys and sometimes they went to be with their mom. I really liked my step sons and they respected me and their mom. We became friends and we all love each other to this day. God is just so awesome. He takes a mountain and makes a crossroad from it. A person, who holds the cross dear, understands that. Out of the most unlikely things, something blooms like a pretty rose in His garden basket of special gifts.

In 1976, while living in Raeford, we attended a precious country Baptist church. We loved the pastor and his wife, Alton and Peggy Smith. They loved the Lord and were foster parents. Alton had a lazy eye and he'd tilt his good eye up towards Heaven, and deliver a sermon that would get you ready to see Jesus burst through the Eastern sky. If he didn't reach you, then you couldn't possibly be alive. They were such dear people. Occasionally I'd discover the rent had been paid. Big boxes of food would be out on our step for Thanksgiving.

One day Peggy said, "Shirley, are you saved?" I had no idea what she meant. She had a little half smile on her face and said, "Well Honey, if you don't know what it means, than you definitely aren't." The tiny little unpretentious church, small in stature and taller than any I've ever known in true spirit, led me to become saved. I was baptized. It was a big turning point in my life. For as much church attendance as I had, I never gave my soul to the Lord, asked Him to keep it, and bring me to Heaven with Him someday. I did that day. On my knees sincerely and humbly, I prayed. I was born again, not to Mary and Walter, but to God through Jesus and His Holy Spirit. I now had humility, true humility. I asked for God's forgiveness of all my sins.

We left Raeford and moved to the Carolina coast to a little beach called Holdens. My husband would have severe chest pains and ended up at Duke University for open heart surgery. He was weak when he came home, and I would sit up all night tending to his incision, and keeping his spirit up. I was really close to him and thought the world of him. I'd walk with him up and down the street to regain his strength and continued babysitting and cleaning houses.

I always tended to be rather reclusive and private. With my husband sick and not working and me baby sitting, I didn't get out of the house much. My neighbor, Ruth Fulford, was very kind. She asked me to go across the street to meet her daughter, Sandra. There I found a life long friend and adopted sister. We always said God put us together for some reason and we stayed in touch even from three thousands miles away.

My husband decided we'd move to Charlotte, North Carolina to be near his sister. My son and daughter were still with us. We attended a good church where people have gigantic hearts to help others. I could barely smile from abscessed and broken teeth, as I had no money to secure good medical or dental help. God bless Sarah, a church member. She took me and had my teeth fixed, then took a church photo of me wearing a beaming smile. I was so proud of my sparkling white teeth. Well, you know who sent her. We are His hands and feet. She was willing. I thought, if life is this beautiful with mountains, rainbows, water falls, and babies, Heaven must be exquisite and a thousand times more marvelous.

In 1980, my daughter, Tara, got married. My son Rhon still lived with us. He was around sixteen years old and had a good and generous heart. He did odd jobs, and mowed grass to bring home money to help, and always did support me and his sisters until he grew up and moved to New Jersey. Darise was ten years of age at this time.

I decided while in Charlotte that I would apply for a grant to continue my education. I was in my mid forties at the time. My husband was at home and could get my daughter to school and back. I received the grant and started a career in early education. To my surprise, I got top grades, mostly A's. I attended Central Piedmont Community College, and was a very motivated student. I worked some mornings at a school called Kiddy Korner and I started in the baby room with six month to one year olds.

God knew this day was very special. Sometimes I'd stay in the room to eat, but this day I ran home on my lunch hour. When I got in, I saw a letter on the table that Charles had set up against the napkin holder so I wouldn't miss it. There it was, a letter from my brother, Walter Paul, and post marked California. My heart sped up. I tore it open so fast I was concerned I had ripped it. I remember blinking back tears in disbelief. Was this really happening?

Rhon's uncle, Walter Paul, had located him through his father's side of the family. He had talked to Rhon a long time and got my telephone number and address. To say I was in shock was putting it mildly. The letter said he and my father had been trying to find me for years, and that my father had a letter on the way also. I went back to school on a cloud. As I'd rock my babies, my mind would be dancing and spinning like a top. It was a thrilling thought that at age forty five, I would soon meet my very own father and brother.

My mind was buzzing with a million questions, and I had enough presence of mind to write them down once my babies all got to sleep. The first questions that I have waited forty five years to ask, "Why didn't you come to see me?" "Didn't you care?" I did have questions, but no anger or animosity. I was in awe. Whoever he was, he made me and gave me my life.

The next day my father sent a darling letter. It would melt any heart. My brother called that evening. We talked the entire night long. He said he had a surprise in the mail. I said to my husband, "I've waited so long, would you be willing to travel out to California for a few weeks?" He said, "I'll do better than that, we'll move out there." He was stationed in San Pedro in the Navy, and loved California. He said he'd love to live back there.

The next letter from my father came within a few days from my conversation with Walt. In the envelope were tickets for me and Darise to go to California within a week. He said he would make arrangements for Charles, Darise and me to rent a house next door and would get us all a moving out ticket later. Everything was perfect! We were packing and so excited. My brother said we would go to Hollywood where he was a record producer, and visit Disneyland. When we got as far as Colorado, I noticed the beautiful mountains. I felt so close to God. My brother had chosen a time that wouldn't offend my parents as they were now deceased.

Words cannot express what I felt when the plane landed in Ontario, California. My daughter, all smiles and full of anticipation, said, "Hurry, Mom, come on, Mom." For some reason, I felt so frightened and nervous about leaving the plane. I didn't know if I'd find an alcoholic father, but I did know he was looking forward to seeing me. His heart was open to me. I must have put on lipstick and perfume three times and combed my hair twice. Finally, I just hopped up and went out the plane door, smiling and looking out. We were out on the tarmac and suddenly as I was coming down the steps in the bright California sun, I saw my daddy and brother outside the terminal crying like babies. We all ran to each other. My brother looked towards heaven and said, "This is for you, Mother, your baby is home." We must have stood out there for thirty minutes bawling and hugging before we could move into the terminal. My dad shocked me because he was so youthful and young looking. I had expected him to be a fragile old man. He wore bold colors, grey slacks, red shirt, and acted years younger than he was. He was in his late seventies at the time. He grabbed my hand and didn't very often let go unless he had to eat or drink coffee. He acted like I had fallen from heaven. He adored me.

We went to a restaurant where I also got acquainted with my brother, Walter Paul. He went back in his mind to the day Mother died when he was just a small boy. He tried so hard to make her real to me. I listened intently as I was so interested in knowing everything. He called me "Baby Sister" even though I was heading towards fifty years old. He had made a family tree dating back to the

1600's. I was so fascinated being with Dad. I just sat anywhere he was, and he was cuddly, warm and affectionate. It was like he couldn't show me enough love. He never did say anything negative about my aunt and uncle. He said he had imagined they were happy, because after all they had me! The way he said it, made me sound like such a treasure and a gift to them.

Mostly, we couldn't take our eyes off each other, and in fact, we were close to mirror image. Daddy had beautiful, thick, white hair, ocean blue eyes, and dimples. He had a tan from California living. He belied his age.

I was told by Walter Paul our ancestry was French English predominately with a tiny bit of Irish. Years ago I had named one child Irish, Tara; one child English, Rhon; and Darise, French. That gave me a chill.

Still, looking strong, but emotionally fragile, I tried to protect my heart for the answer I would receive when I looked straight into my father's face and said, "Dad, I've got to say this, I was always hurt you never wrote me or came to see me." His eyes showed sadness in them. He was drinking coffee. He put his cup down, took my hand, and turned towards me. He said, "I have loved all my children all my life. Honey, you were my baby. I did come to see you." My brother interrupted, "I was with him once." "I got remarried, your aunt didn't approve of me or the marriage, and I was always given an excuse by her or a threat by your uncle. I was poor and they had influence and money. I am not a type of person to fight and fuss. I had nothing against them, they were good people. After years of this, I just thought you would be better off and have a better life without me." I guess the look on my face made him say, "You didn't know did you?" I told him, "No, I didn't". Then the words of unmistaken truth, "I guess I should have tried harder and I am sorry."

We spent hours and hours talking and looking at old pictures. This was a pivotal moment in my life. I finally knew who I was. The girl who knew nothing had full knowledge now. My father explained his people were from LaRochelle, France, a fishing port, and his great grandfather had built his own ship to carry his family to England. They were French Huguenots and persecuted and even killed for their faith. They were people of strong faith and were very resourceful, and so is Shirley, I thought. It was the first time I felt truly proud to be a Marriner.

I still wondered why there was no support, school clothes, birthday cards, gifts or phone calls. This all equaled no love in my mind, but it was impossible to hate this man. His flesh and blood God used to create me. He reached my heart. He was a sweet man, very lovable, extremely kind, and just of a happy go lucky nature. Was he a role model parent? No. He was far from it. I know that. I wanted a dad on a white horse charging in to head up his family, and this my father was not. I could see so much of my own personality in him. He was uneducated, but not insensitive. I had always been a mild passive personality myself. I couldn't judge any mistakes of his because God says honor your mother and father. It was actually easy for me to honor him. I understood him so well.

My brother, a few years older than I, was mentally ill and institutionalized. I said, "Daddy, why didn't you go to visit Marty?" He got tears and replied, "Aw Hon, honestly? It hurt too much. It was Hell to see him in there. I couldn't get him out, and all those people screaming made it awful. I couldn't stand him being there." He said, "I hated he was there, but I knew he got the help and care he needed." What parent leaves a child abandoned? I chose to see his heart which was sincere by the way he thought about things. It didn't make it right, but it showed how he coped with situations.

My sister would feel much differently. To her, our father seemed like a monster who showed no compassion, support, or caring to children who didn't ask to be born. My aunt felt that way and probably tried to protect me and my sister from him. To me, my sister was a blessing and God send. While I understand my sister and aunt's feelings, this is my experience.

I write it from my perspective even though I respect their right to those feelings, too.

Dad would tell me that my Grandfather Marriner ruled with a strong voice and heavy hand. He had hands the size of a giant. A few swats and Daddy would nearly be sent half way across the room. He adored his parents. Grandmother Marriner was a little sweetheart and spoiled him a lot. One time, when I was about fifteen years old, my sister slipped me down to Farmingdale to meet my grandparents. The first thing I noticed about Grandpop was his huge hands and height of about 6'4. He was a very emotional man too. He got out his white hanky and cried the entire time I was there. He was so thrilled to see me. He and my grandmother were such a cute couple. She was around 5' tall and he was fiercely protective. She'd had thirty mini strokes and we couldn't surprise her by coming too close too fast. We were only there for a half hour, but it was thrilling. I left my grandfather with a wet hanky from tears of love. My sister made me promise I wouldn't tell, as she felt so much love and loyalty to our parents. Grandpop said, "I don't know what they have been telling you down there, but don't feel hard towards your daddy. He is a good boy, great son, and never gave us any trouble."

When Daddy told me about the hands, I certainly knew exactly what he meant. Brother Walt said, "Yeah, if I got drunk, Grandpop would skin my hide." Dad would say, "Junior come lay down, I'll get you a pan if you get sick, and I'm just glad you weren't killed.

My daughter was quite taken with her new grandfather and was spoiled a lot by him. She spent a lot of time with him and enjoyed having a grandfather. They would have yard sales and he would tease and talk with her. She felt close to him and that was nice because she was very young when my parents died. He was jolly and funny. He would make her laugh. He loved to cook for Darise and me. He would come over a lot and make great dinners and serve us like we were stars. I really enjoyed the times I was Dad's most special guest while he poured love and attention on me.

My husband Charles was good to my dad, and my dad thanked him for bringing me out to California. As my husband wished, my brother and sister-in-law gave him the money for security officer school. They bought him books, uniforms and a gun. We were all happy in California. Darise was fifteen years old, and made some nice school friends. California looked so very beautiful.

I wanted some quiet time with Daddy alone. I asked him to sit on the steps of our porch and tell me all about my mother. Anything I would ask, he would be so happy to share. Daddy began, "Your mother was from good people. They were church people. I liked Harry Gravatt, my father-in-law, and he was a good man, too. Your mother's mother was a good lady and her side was English. She was brought up in a loving home. They were Methodist people. Your mother was born in Belmar, New Jersey and she loved her family more than anything." He spoke so lovingly of her. He said if she had lived they would be together today.

He told me about the day he was walking down the street in Englishtown, New Jersey and looked into a window at Woolworths and saw the most beautiful creature—my mom. He went in there buying things every day until he worked up the courage to ask her out. He said she was a living dream. She had auburn hair and warm blue green eyes with a personality and body to match. Evidently, Daddy swept her off her feet. He went into Woolworths one day, mother quit and they ran off to Elkton, MD to get married. Then along came the five of us. He said she loved being a mother. The light in his eyes touched me when he spoke of my mother. It was wonderful to know I'd been born from so much love. That time on the porch endeared my father to me. I admired the way he respected my mother. His eyes were full of love for the memory he was sharing with me, their daughter.

Daddy explained that my mother's people lived in London and Durham. He said many were creative or musical. He spoke of my redheaded great, great grandmother who was a twin. They came across to America and were the sweethearts of the cruise trip. Both were stylish, pleasant, and loved to dance and entertain. They were singers and celebrated with all the passengers.

Dad had questions, too. Did I ever go near Farmingdale with my aunt and uncle because he was there for years and so were my grandparents. His parents had a camp called, "Fresh Air Kids." Children from New York would come out for the summers. Grandpop and Grandmom spoiled them, and they hated to return to the city. They taught them fishing and carpentry. Grandmother taught the children how to sew and make crafts. Daddy was proud of the men in his family ancestry. Some were sea captains because La Rochelle was a fishing port. Some were whalers, all great cooks, and others musicians. One was an orchestra leader. I thought they left me quite an inheritance. I admired them all.

Both my father and brother died close together. Shortly before their passing, my brother said, "Sis, find a good man and be happy." My husband, Charles, had left me for a twenty two year old woman, and my daughter and I were evicted from our home. He'd taken money I'd worked for, and did not pay the rent. Instead, he gave it to his new love. I was absolutely destroyed. The thing which broke me so much was that he stole my beautiful charm bracelet that I cherished with my babies' birth charms. I couldn't get it back. He took it into a pawn shop and they had already sold it. I felt like I was walking around with a hole in my heart. My Father in Heaven picked up the broken pieces of my life and sent a church to pay the first months rent. My daughter and I had a place to live. He took care of us like always.

At least Daddy, Walt and I made our time count. In God's perfect timing, I got to spend time with them before they passed away. Dad died first and brother nearly grieved himself too death over his loss. He had stayed close to Daddy. In my analysis of myself, I always thought I was a nobody. The whole time I was God's daughter born from love with a rich history. Everyone needs a strong sense of self. Once I knew my background, I felt lifted up and content. Consider, God, although I couldn't see my father and brother, they did exist. They were there. It's the same with faith.

I married twice in California after Charles, once to a sweet man who was a Mormon. We were deeply close as friends, but we were too incompatible in our religious beliefs. We parted but remain friends.

An older man entered my life, and he was a dear person sixteen years older. Was I still looking for a father? He was the kindest man I had ever met up to that point. He was healthy and active for three years. He worried about my life and wanted me to have money when I grew older for security. He turned over IRA's and our home to me as he wanted to take care of me.

He developed Alzheimer's became physically abusive. I know he would never have wanted to harm me. He had dementia and could not help it.

I had to put him in an Alzheimer's unit because he would wander and could hurt himself. I took a trip back East, and when I returned, everything was stolen. All of my special gifts from my children and grandchildren were gone including a mother's ring, grandmother's quilts, and everything I loved and admired from my family. Someone brought a charge against me in court stating I forced my husband to give me our home when he wasn't clear in his mind. But, he was. It was his idea. From our first year together he had said, "I want you to have security for later. I want to take care of you." The lawyer made sure of this by asking very specific questions. His mind would have had to be sharp to answer. I ended up losing my home, all of my belongings, and most of the money because of lawyer fees. My husband had given from his heart because he felt sad over my life. He later died and my family and I felt very badly. We knew the truth. At least I had the honor of knowing a truly good man who loved me and tried to take care of me.

I was reflecting one day as to how fast my life had gone by. Here I was in California, almost sixty years old and a grandmother to five. Just then the phone rang and it was my adopted sister, Sandra. It was her mother who brought me across the street to introduce us years ago. We had stayed close.

She asked me to please come out for her birthday. We hadn't seen each other in years and would I please come. I took my vacation from teaching preschool, and bought my ticket. We were so excited to reunite.

I arrived, and as girl friends do, I shared my heart with her. I was telling her how my dreams were unfulfilled and I was worn out from life. I was tired and drained. All my past relationships seemed to be me giving and giving all I had: love, money, affection, and nursing care - only to lose. I felt frustrated as I was a failure at marriage. Did I place a man up too high? Had I put him above God? Was that why? She said, "Sis, I know. Let's go out and get a nice seafood dinner." We planned to go to a lovely restaurant on Sunset Beach. She could always pick me up and make me smile. She suggested we take her brother Robert with us. She asked if I minded. I knew of Robert, but didn't know him personally. I had heard what a wonderful brother he was. I knew if she needed anything, he would help her and be there for whatever she needed. Years ago his mother told me about her children and she adored Robert. He was a devoted son, brother, and dad, but that's all I knew. We were distant acquaintances, so I believed him to be simply a nice man.

We were in a red convertible and his niece was up front with her mother. He and I rode in the back seat. I was to learn first hand that he was also a gentleman. When we arrived, he helped me out of the car and pulled my chair out for me at dinner. I must say he was completely captivating. Something happened that evening that made the two of us magnets. We could not be apart after that. It was like God had joined us together. We got back in the car and my hair was flying all over because the top was down. He went to pull my hair back from my face and his hand brushed my cheek. I knew I would love him forever. He felt the same. In our wildest dreams we never could have known we would find the deepest and greatest love of our lives that night. We sat in the back seat of the car, under the moon and stars, talking until morning.

The next night, we walked on the beach where he gathered sand shells where my foot steps walked. He gathered them and traced my foot print on a manila folder, glued the sand to my foot silhouette, and then painted my nails on the foot cut out in my favorite color purple. He attached the little shells and painted them purple, hanging them from the heels. It was the most thoughtful and touching thing a man ever did for me. He melted my heart. He was miserable when I went back to California. I was miserable too. He lit a candle for me every night I was away.

So, he hopped on a train, rented a U-Haul truck, packed up my belongings and my little white Toyota, and brought me back to marry him on Holden Beach. I had a very serious talk with him. I told him he would have to promise never to hurt or cheat on me. I was much older now and would be leaving everyone in my family and was honestly afraid. He said, "God gave me an angel with a broken wing, I know my part and I won't ever hurt or leave you." He had been hurt too, but God showed us we could make it.

When we aren't looking and seeking, God sends us the perfect match. I think God loves surprises. God hand picked Robert because he could give the love, support and guidance I had always needed. I could do the same for him. That was five years ago and he's kept his word. His hands have never hurt me. His heart is mine. We put God at the Head of us. We got married in a little church, in a candlelight service. I could feel God tying our knot. I have never had a happier day. He is the best man I have ever been honored to know. He shows me every day how he loves and adores me.

I have lost many things, but I have a goldmine in Heavenly treasures. They are worth much more than anything on earth. My lovely neighbor of the past, Robert's mother, became my mother-in-law. She is deceased, but I know she would have been so pleased and happy for us. My adopted sister Sandra is now my sister-in-law.

I have been out of God's will, but never out of His grip. I am so very blessed. I am wealthy in faith, family and friends. We had both lost everything financially. By the world's standards we are poor, but we count wealth differently. We know what God gave us and what we found. I must have favor with God. I have lived my mother's lifetime twice. I found what true love really means. I have healthy, beautiful children and grandchildren. I enjoy good health. I have found and received all I yearned for. How could I ask for more? Many good friends are devoted to me and their love has carried me through some very hard times. My sister has been the best mother and friend. Sandra has been a sister and sister-in-law. Betty is a dear and close friend. Amelia's been my caretaker. Lucy has been my prayer partner. Nancy, Ruth, and Billie Ann have given love and support when I truly needed them. They all lift my heart and I thank God for them.

So, who is Shirley? I am a sincere God fearing lady. A good soul who has lived an amazing life, soaring up to the top of high heights and falling painfully way down to the lowest, degrading, and demeaning places. I learned through many bitter tears and a lot of sorrow and disappointments that the true source of love can only be found in Jesus' presence through the Holy Spirit of God. His love will never fail you. I truly know for I have lived it.

I am part angel, and at times devilish. I am very sensitive, tender hearted, and humorous. I am mother, daughter, sister, friend, aunt and Miss Shirley to hundreds of children. I am grandmother, sweetheart and wife. I am a child of the King.

Many times the devil would distract and trap me. I'd be on the wrong road. He is very good at enticing and destroying. He uses bait that is very desirable, hooks you, and you go spinning in a fast, descending spiral downward where you hit bottom. He is very clever and you must stay aware and one up on him. The way to do it is stay close to the Lord. Love is your defense. Life is yours and it's a most privileged gift. Jesus showed us His supreme sacrifice of love so we could spend our years in peace and hope. I let the devil rob me sometimes. Don't let him rob you. I grew from a tormented, sad little girl chasing snowflakes through the whipping winds of childhood to becoming a strong spirited Christian woman who loves Jesus above all else.

I want my life to help others and stand for something good as a witness and testimony to what you can endure with faith. Live with it. Die with it. I would not have made it through my life, had I not had it. I want to encourage and give you hope. Please learn from my mistakes. Life can be serene with Jesus' strength. Suffering makes you stronger and much more compassionate in life. It helps you grow spiritually. Loss and poverty gives you humility and makes you humble and appreciative. I went through hell and came out in heaven. I am not lost anymore. The search is over!

Author's Biography

At the age of sixty-four, this is Shirley Fulford's first attempt at becoming an author by telling her life's experiences, both the joyful and the tragic.

She was born in Middlesex County at Middlesex General Hospital, New Brunswick, New Jersey, and raised just outside of Princeton. Her family was scattered when she was two and a half years old.

Throughout her childhood she was intrigued with poetry, reading, writing, art, music, and painting. She was encouraged to look things up in the dictionary, and the encyclopedias never gathered dust upstairs on the shelf in her home. This gave Shirley a zest for learning, and what she found as a child, led her to an early love for words.

The traumatic early loss of her mother, and the separation from her father and brothers, left her with emptiness and many self identity issues. Curiosity followed her throughout adolescence and into adult life.

She struggled through a secretive, lonely childhood to become a strong woman of faith who learned about life the hard way, and survived it.

Life's trials and tribulations caused an endless void, and yet a resolution that was so totally fulfilling has compelled her to take you on the voyage of hardship and a faith that could only have been given by her Lord and Savior, Jesus Christ.

She expresses love and gratitude to husband Robert, daughters Tara Lynne and Darise Alene, son Rhon, grandchildren Starla, Skyla, Dalayna, Hunter, and Aubrey just for living and sharing life on the road she has traveled.